ANIMALS ARE AMAZING

TIGERS

BY VALERIE BODDEN

This edition published in the UK in 2014 by
Franklin Watts
338 Euston Road
London NW1 3BH

Franklin Watts Australia
Level 17/207 Kent Street
Sydney NSW 2000

First published by Creative Education,
an imprint of the Creative Company.
Copyright © 2010 and 2012 Creative Education
International copyright reserved in all countries.
No part of this book may be reproduced in any
form without written permission from the publisher.

ISBN: 978 1 4451 2956 3
Dewey number: 599.7'56

A CIP catalogue record for this book
is available from the British Library.

Printed in China

Franklin Watts is a division of
Hachette Children's Books
an Hachette UK company
www.hachette.co.uk

Book and cover design by The Design Lab
Art direction by Rita Marshall

Photographs by 123RF (Nattthawat Wongrat),
Corbis (John Conrad, Randy Wells), Dreamstime
(Napy8gen), Getty Images (Theo Allofs, Altrendo
Nature, Chris Baker, P. Kumar, Thorsten Milse,
Schafer & Hill, Gary Vestal), iStockphoto (Vinod
Bartakk, Derek Dammann, Eric Isselee, Keith
Livingston)

CONTENTS

What are tigers?   4
Tiger facts   7
Big cats   8
Where tigers live   11
Tiger food   12
New tigers   15
Hunting for food   16
Tiger sounds   19
Tigers and people   20
A tiger story   22
Useful information   24

What are tigers?

Tigers are the largest wild cats in the world. There are six **species** of tiger in the wild. There used to be nine species, but three of them are now **extinct**.

Tigers have striped fur and white spots on their ears.

species different types of an animal that all share the same name.
extinct something that has died out and will never be alive again.

Tiger facts

Most tigers are orange with black stripes. Some tigers are white with black stripes. All tigers have white fur on their belly, throat, and legs. Tigers have very big teeth. They also have long, sharp claws. They have whiskers too, just like a pet cat.

Every tiger has a different pattern of stripes. No two are the same.

Big cats

Tigers can grow to be over three metres long. If a tiger stood up on its back legs, it would be much taller than a grown-up man! Male tigers can weigh more than 250 kilogrammes. A female tiger is usually smaller. She is called a tigress.

Tigers are fierce but they also like to play.

Where tigers live

*Tigers in the wild all live on the **continent** of Asia.*

Some tigers live in cold, snowy forests. They have much thicker fur to protect them from the cold. Other tigers live in rainforests or warm **swamps**. All tigers can swim. They are the only big cat that likes to get wet!

continent one of Earth's seven big pieces of land.
swamps areas of land that are covered with water and trees.

Tiger food

All tigers eat meat. Their favourite foods are deer and wild pigs, but tigers have even eaten people! A tiger can eat up to 40 kilogrammes of food at a time. After they have eaten, they cover up the rest of their dinner with grass or leaves.

Tigers sometimes share their food with other tigers.

New tigers

A tigress will have two to six cubs at a time. The cubs drink their mother's milk for the first few months. The cubs grow very quickly. She teaches them to hunt when they are older and stronger. Cubs leave their mother by the time they are three years old. Wild tigers can live for more than 20 years.

Tigers have blue or green eyes when they are cubs. Most adult tigers have amber eyes.

cubs baby tigers.

Hunting for food

Adult tigers like to live and hunt alone. They sleep for most of the day and usually hunt for **prey** at night. Tigers creep up behind their prey and then pounce! A tiger's stripes help to **camouflage** it in long grass and in forests. This makes it hard for prey animals to see tigers.

Tigers sometimes hide in long grass to camouflage themselves.

prey animals that are eaten by other animals.
camouflage a pattern on an animal's fur or skin that helps it to blend in with grass, bushes, trees or other habitats.

Tiger sounds

Tigers can make many different sounds. They can make a quiet "chuff" sound through their noses. They can also growl, snarl and hiss. Tigers roar very loudly – it can be heard up to two kilometres away.

Tigers may roar to tell other tigers to stay away.

Tigers and people

Today, some tigers are kept in zoos. Tigers are an **endangered** species and zoos help to breed more tigers. These tigers are often released back into the wild. People all over the world like to watch tigers. It is exciting to see these big cats eat, sleep and play!

Many people go to zoos to see tigers and other big cats.

endangered an animal or plant that only has a small number of them left on Earth.

A tiger story

Why do tigers have stripes? People in Asia tell a story about this. They say that the tiger asked a man for wisdom. The man said he had to go and get the wisdom. He did not want the tiger to eat his animals while he was gone, so he used ropes to tie the tiger to a tree. When the man came back he had an armful of straw. He lit a fire under the tiger with the straw to teach him about wisdom. The tiger escaped but the fire burned his fur and left black stipes on it.

Useful information

Read More

Leapfrog Learners: Big Cats by Annabelle Lynch
(Franklin Watts, 2013)

Animal Attack: Killer Cats by Alex Woolf (Franklin Watts, 2014)

Amazing Animals: Tigers by Sally Morgan (Franklin Watts, 2013)

Websites

http://kids.nationalgeographic.com/kids/animals/creaturefeature/tiger/
This site has lots of facts about tigers, photos and a film of a tiger
taking a bath.

http://www.activityvillage.co.uk/tigers.htm
This site has lots of tiger related craft and colouring activities
for children.

Every effort has been made by the Publishers to ensure that these websites are suitable
for children, that they are of the highest educational value and that they contain no
inappropriate or offensive material. However, because of the nature of the Internet, it
is impossible to guarantee that the contents of these sites will not be altered. We strongly
advise that Internet access is supervised by a responsible adult.

Index

Asia 11, 22
claws 7
colours 7
continents 11
cubs 15
endangered 20

food 12, 15, 16
forests 11, 16
fur 4, 7, 11, 16, 22
hunting 15, 16
rainforest 11
size 8
sounds 19

species 4, 20
stripes 4, 7, 16, 22
swamps 11
swimming 11
teeth 7
tigress 8, 15
zoos 20